Theory for Young Musicians

Games & Exercises to Enhance Music Skills

Carla Ulbrich

ISBN-10: 0-7390-0231-7
ISBN-13: 978-0-7390-0231-5

Cover Photos
Violin courtesy of Scherl & Roth/United Musical Instruments, U.S.A., Inc.
Guitar courtesy of Martin Guitar Company
Boy, lower left: © 2001 RubberBall Productions

Alfred Music
P.O. Box 10003
Van Nuys, CA 91410-0003
alfred.com

Table of Contents

About the Author

Photo by Mickey Romeo

A Clemson, South Carolina native, Carla Ulbrich began studying classical guitar at the age of nine. She studied piano, clarinet, piccolo, flute and tuba while in school. All the while, she continued her guitar playing and discovered her songwriting abilities during her first year of college. She has a bachelor's degree in music and has taught guitar at North Greenville College and Lander University, her own teaching studio and at the National Guitar Workshop.

Her songwriting and guitar playing have landed her numerous honors, including: First place, 2000 Mid-Atlantic Song Contest; Best Upbeat and Best Overall, 1999 South Florida Folk Fest Song Competition; First Place, 1998 Mid-Atlantic Songwriting Contest (open category); Fourth most requested on Dr. Demento; and a grant from the South Carolina Arts Commission. She performs as a solo act all over the East Coast, making numerous TV and radio appearances along the way, and has shared the bill with such luminaries as Cheryl Wheeler and Twiggy the Water Skiing Squirrel. Carla Ulbrich is a member of ASCAP, likes cheese and collects bottlecaps. Learn more at www.carlau.com.

About This Book

This is a book to write in. You will learn the names of the notes for both the treble clef and the bass clef. You will also learn how to write the notes. If you are learning an instrument, you should also have a book that has basic instruction and pieces of music for you to play.

You will find three things in this book: Stories, Lightning Rounds and recipes. You will complete the stories by writing notes or note names; Lightning Rounds are quizzes; and the recipes give you another fun way to use what you know about music. Have fun!

Two Important Things to Know Before You Start

There are two things you can tell about a note by looking at it:

1)   How long or short it is (its rhythm)

2)   How high or low it is (its pitch)

Rhythm

You can tell how long or short a note is (its rhythm) by its shape.

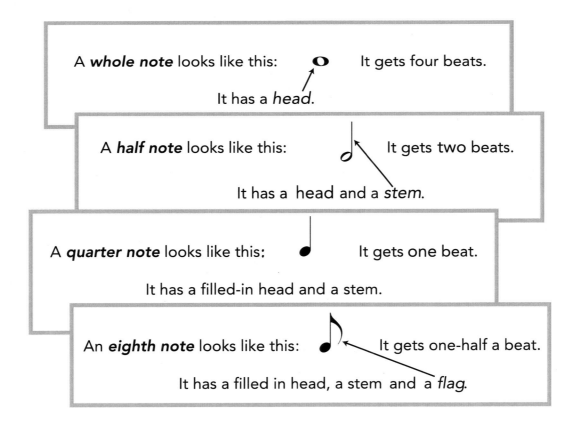

A **whole note** looks like this: **O**   It gets four beats.
It has a *head*.

A **half note** looks like this: It gets two beats.
It has a head and a *stem*.

A **quarter note** looks like this: It gets one beat.
It has a filled-in head and a stem.

An **eighth note** looks like this: It gets one-half a beat.
It has a filled in head, a stem and a *flag*.

Pitch

Music is written on a group of five lines, called a *staff*. It looks like this.

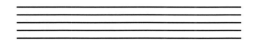

You can tell how high or low a note is by where it is on the staff.

High note

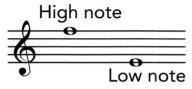

Low note

The notes are given letter names, using the first seven letters of the alphabet.
A B C D E F G

Treble Clef

This is a *treble clef*.  Here it is on a staff.

When there is a treble clef on the staff, the names of the notes are:

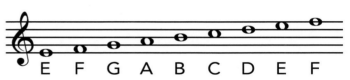

E F G A B C D E F

You can remember the names of the treble clef notes on the lines with this saying:
Every Good Boy Does Fine

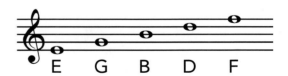

E   G   B   D   F

The notes that are in the spaces of the treble clef spell the word **FACE**.

F   A   C   E

Some of the instruments that play music written in the treble clef are: Flute, violin, guitar, clarinet and piano (right hand).

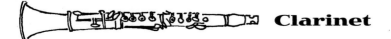 **Flute**

Clarinet

 **Violin**

This is a **bass clef.** 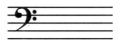 Here it is on the staff.

When there is a bass clef on the staff, the names of the notes are:

G A B C D E F G A

You can remember the names of the bass clef notes on the lines with this saying: **G**ood **B**oys **D**o **F**ine **A**lways

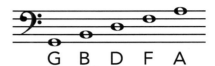

G B D F A

You can remember the notes in the spaces of the bass clef with this saying: **A**ll **C**ows **E**at **G**rass.

A C E G

Some of the instruments that play music written in the bass clef are: Tuba, bass, trombone, bassoon, cello and piano (left hand). These instruments play lower pitches than the treble clef instruments.

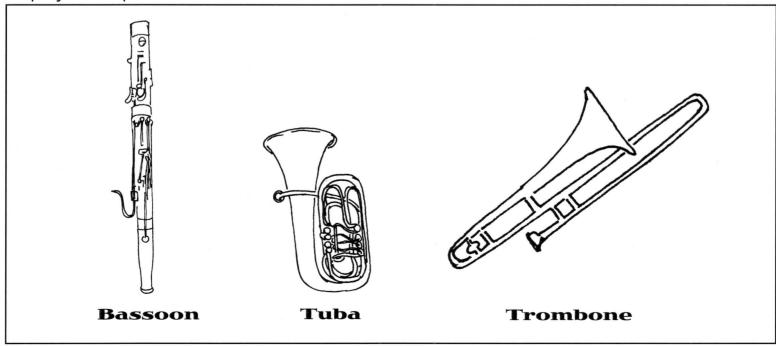

Bassoon   **Tuba**   **Trombone**

Stems

For notes that have stems (half notes, quarter notes, eighth notes), the stem goes up and on the right side for notes below the third line of any staff. This is true in both the treble and bass clefs.

The stem goes down and to the left for notes on the third line of any staff and above. This is also true in both clefs.

Flags

For notes with flags (eighth notes), the flag always goes to the right of the stem.

Accidentals

Sometimes a note will have a **flat (♭)** or a **sharp (♯)** in front of it. The flat or sharp is placed on the same line or space as the note. The note in *Example 1* would be called "C-sharp" and the note in *Example 2* would be called "B-flat."

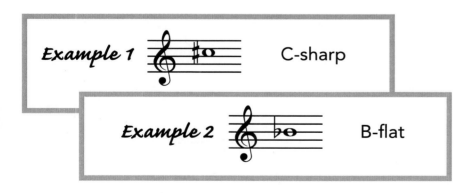

Example 1   C-sharp

Example 2   B-flat

Slick In Trouble

Treble Clef

Name the notes to spell words that complete the story.
Write each letter name on the line below the note. Here is an example:

Slick, the cat, was diving into  paper . He knocked over

ex — a

ex — b a g

 of toys and made  line for the

1 — _ _ _

2 — _ _

3 — _ _ _

Note: These gray numbers will help you
find the correct answers on the answer pages
at the back of the book.

goldfish. 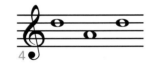 grabbed Slick and threw him outside. Slick

4 — _ _ _

 and  to  let in.

5 — _ _ _ _ _

6 — _ _ _ _ _

7 — _ _

"  , 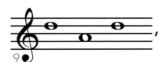 , look at that  ."

8 — _ _ _

9 — _ _ _

10 — _ _ _ _

Recipe No. 1—Cookies

Draw the type of note that gets the same number of beats the recipe uses for indgredients. Have your parents help you with the oven.

(lb. = pound, c. = cup, tsp. = teaspoon)

Example

½ 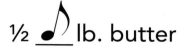 lb. butter

2 ½ ___ + ___ c. flour
  6   7

Continue

1 ___ c. dark brown sugar
  1

1 ___ tsp. salt
  8

1 ___ c. granulated sugar
  2

1 ___ tsp. baking soda
  9

1 ___ egg
  3

1 ___ c. nuts (optional)
  10

1 ½ ___ + ___ tsp. vanilla
    4   5

2 ___ c. chocolate chips
  11

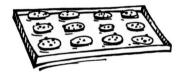

Mix all ingredients together. Separate into small balls of dough on cookie sheet.

Bake 8–10 minutes at 375° F.

A Typical Day with Slick

Treble Clef

Spell the underlined words with notes. Use whole notes. When there are
two ways to write a note on the staff, either way will be correct.*

Slick has [1] added [2] a lot to my life. He likes to [3] be

[4] fed and [5] fed and [6] fed. On [7] a busy day, he will

walk on the piano, play with [8] a [9] bag, sleep in [10] baggage,

chase [11] a [12] bead across the floor, hang over the [13] edge

of the deck, [14] beg to [15] be [16] fed, stick his

[17] face under my hand and hide under the

[18] bed and playfully attack me with [19] a-sharp claw.

* The answer page will show both correct answers.

Recipe No. 2—Way Too Much Frosting

Fill in the total number of beats these notes add up to.
(c. = cup, tbsp. = tablespoon, tsp. = teaspoon)

_____ 𝅝 + 𝅗𝅥 c. brown sugar
1

_____ 𝅗𝅥 + 𝅘𝅥 c. sugar
2

_____ 𝅝 + 𝅝 + 𝅝 tbsp. butter
3

_____ 𝅝 + 𝅗𝅥 tbsp. corn syrup
4

_____ 𝅘𝅥𝅮 tsp. salt
5

_____ 𝅗𝅥 + 𝅝 tsp. vanilla
6

_____ 𝅗𝅥 c. milk
7

Road Trip

Treble Clef
Name the notes to spell missing words, and spell
underlined words by drawing notes on the staff.
Use whole notes. Watch for accidentals!

and _____ went on _____ road trip.

had _____ brother in Dover, _____. They traveled from Athens,
E d _____ a _____ D E*

_____ , to Dover, _____ . _____ was really hungry. "It's time to
_____ _____ A b e

_____ my _____ !" he _____ .

_____ finally agreed. They found _____ small _____ on
E d _____ a _____ c a f e

* DE = Delaware
** _ _ = Georgia

Lightning Round No. 1

This is a chance for you to test your skills.

Draw eight treble clefs. Draw each one in three strokes, as shown below.

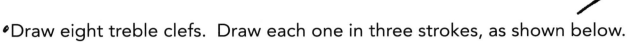

Name the following notes.

Turn these notes into half notes by adding stems to them. Remember: The stem goes up for notes below the third line and down for notes on or above the third line.

Draw a treble clef and write these notes on the staff. Write them as whole notes in the boxes.

Treble Clef   f   g   c   d   a   b   e   g-sharp   d-flat

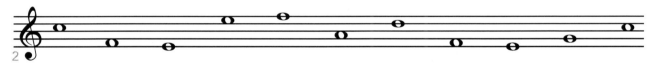

Draw a treble clef and write these notes on the staff. Use half notes. Remember the stem rule.

Treble Clef   a   c   f-sharp   e   b-flat   g   a-flat   d   c-sharp   f

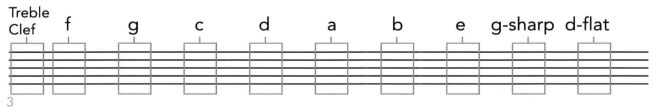

Scavenger Hunt

Bass Clef
Name the notes to complete the story.

At  party on  end street on the

 of town, the host held scavenger hunt. This was the list:

1

2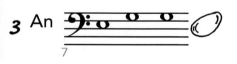

3 An

4 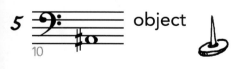 paper

5 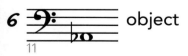 object

6 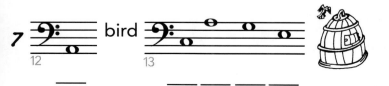 object

7  bird

8  tag

9 Money with  Lincoln on it

10 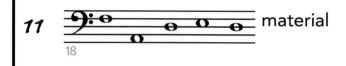 plastic

11 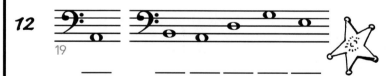 material

12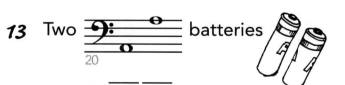

13 Two  batteries

14  menu

15 doll

The Visit

Bass Clef

Spell the underlined words by drawing half notes.
Remember, the stem goes up for notes below the third line,
and goes down for notes on the third line and above.

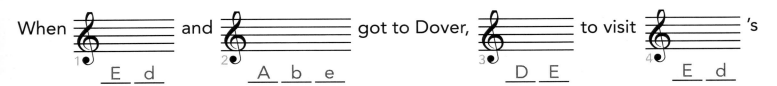

When _E_ _d_ and _A_ _b_ _e_ got to Dover, _D_ _E_ to visit _E_ _d_ 's

brother and his family, _D_ _e_ _e_ _D_ _e_ _e_ was very excited. She wrote to her

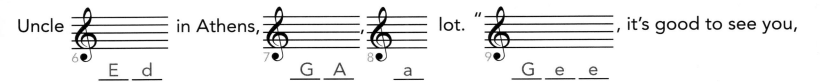

Uncle _E_ _d_ in Athens, _G_ _A_ , _a_ lot. " _G_ _e_ _e_ , it's good to see you,

Uncle _E_ _d_ ," said _D_ _e_ _e_ _D_ _e_ _e_ ." This is my friend, _A_ _b_ _e_ ,"

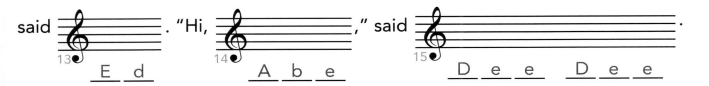

said _E_ _d_ . "Hi, _A_ _b_ _e_ ," said _D_ _e_ _e_ _D_ _e_ _e_ .

"Come on in and I'll show you around. This is your _b_ _e_ _d_ , Uncle _E_ _d_ ,

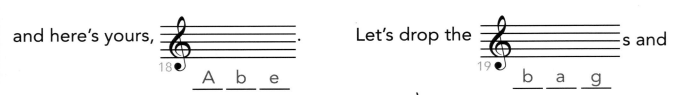

and here's yours, _A_ _b_ _e_ . Let's drop the _b_ _a_ _g_ s and

have dinner."

The Card Game

Bass Clef

Name the notes to spell missing words, and spell
underlined words by drawing notes on the staff.
Use half notes. Remember the stem rule.

After  and her brother went to , her mom

__ __ __ __ __ __   __ __ __

and  stayed up and played card game with  and

__ __ __   __   __ __

. 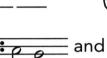 dealt the cards  up, so he had to deal

__ __ __   E d   f a c e

them again, 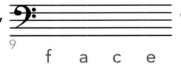 down.  had the  of hearts,

f a c e   E d   a c e

the  of spades and three cards. "Not

a c e   f a c e

 hand," he thought, trying to keep a straight

__   __ __ __

. was winning the game when

__ __ __

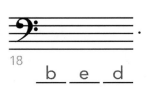's mom suggested they go to .

__ __ __ __ __ __   b e d

17

Lightning Round No. 2

Draw eight bass clefs. Make one big stroke and then surround F, the fourth line from the bottom, with dots, as shown below:

Name these notes:

Draw a bass clef and write these notes on the staff. Use whole notes.

Bass Clef   c   g   a   e   b   f   g   d   c

Add stems to the notes above to change them into half notes.

Name these notes.

Draw a bass clef and write the notes on the staff. Use half notes.

Bass Clef   b   g   c   a   f-sharp   d-flat   e-flat   g-sharp

The Zoo

"Hey Uncle [1]," said [2]," [3]

and [4] went to [5] game. Can we go to the zoo?"

"Sure," said [6]. They took [7]

to the [8] of town. They paid the [9]

to get in, passed the bird [10]s and stopped at

the monkey house. The man wearing [11]

said, "Hi! You're just in time to watch them [12] the monkeys!"

"Oh boy!" [13] said, as her [14] lit up.

A Good Deed

Treble Clef
Spell the underlined words by drawing notes.
Use quarter notes. Remember the stem rule.

On the way home from the zoo, [1] _E d_ and [2] _D e e D e e_ saw an

older woman struggling with [3] _a_ heavy [4] _b a g_. "It's [5] _a_ good day for

[6] _a_ good [7] _d e e d_," said [8] _E d_." That's not [9] _a_ [10] _b a d_

idea," said [11] _D e e D e e_. [12] _E d_ went to the lady and tried to help

with the [13] _b a g_. But, she thought he was [14] _a_ [15] _b a d_ man trying

to steal her bag. Her [16] _f a c e_ turned red and she yelled in [17] _a-sharp_

voice, "Trying to steal my [18] _b a g_, eh?" "I just wanted

to do [19] _a_ good [20] _d e e d_," said Ed.

The Post Office

Bass Clef
Spell the underlined words by drawing notes. Use quarter notes.

𝄢 ____ and 𝄢 ____ stopped by the
1 E d   2 D e e   D e e

Post Office where 𝄢 ____ 's cousin
                  3 D e e   D e e

𝄢 ____ worked. 𝄢 ____ said, "Come
4 D e b   5 D e b

on back and I'll give you a tour. Here's 𝄢 ____
                                          6 a

visitor's 𝄢 ____ . When you put 𝄢 ____ letter in this slot, it lands in
          7 b a d g e   8 a

this 𝄢 ____ tray." 𝄢 ____ and 𝄢 ____ watched as the workers
     9 flat   10 D e e   D e e   11 E d

𝄢 ____ the mail. "Well, I'd love to 𝄢 ____ ," said
12 b a g g e d   13 g a b

𝄢 ____ , "but I better 𝄢 ____ getting back to work."
14 D e b   15 b e

The Story

Bass Clef
Name the notes to complete the story.

"In the year 1877 ," said ,

___ ___   ___ ___

"Thomas Edison invented the record player. There were no 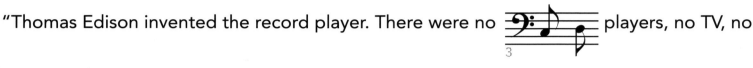 players, no TV, no

___ ___

cassettes." 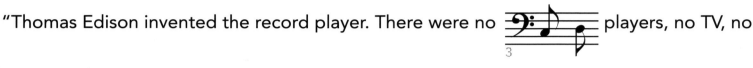 tried to imagine life with no  player

___ ___ ___   ___ ___ ___   ___ ___

and no TV. " , Uncle 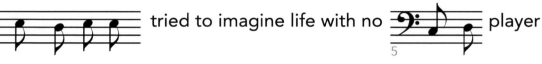, what did people do?" she asked.

___ ___ ___   ___ ___

"Well, , they made their own music," said , and

___ ___ ___ ___ ___ ___ ___   ___ ___

he sang: "  la  la  …" "No, Uncle ," said

___ ___   ___ ___   ___ ___   ___ ___

, "It's  la la la la!"

___ ___ ___ ___ ___ ___ ___   ___ ___ ___

Name the notes.

Turn these note heads into eighth notes by adding stems and flags.

Draw a treble clef and write these notes on the staff. Use quarter notes.

clef   a   c   f   e   b-flat d-sharp g-flat f-sharp a-flat c-sharp

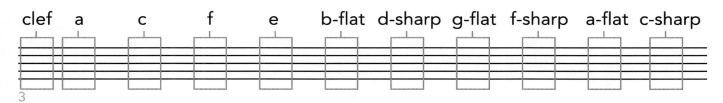

Draw a bass clef and write these notes on the staff. Use quarter notes.

clef   f   e   b   d   a-flat c-sharp f-sharp g-flat   b-flat c-sharp

Change the notes in the line above into eighth notes by adding flags to them.

Treble Clef

Name the notes to spell missing words, and spell underlined words
by drawing notes on the staff. Use eighth notes. Remember the stem rule, and
that the flag is always to the right of the stem.

"Do you know any stories,  ?" asked  .

___ ___ ___   ___ ___ ___ ___

 told them  story about his first job. "When I was

A b e   a

eighteen," said , "I worked as

___ ___ ___   ___ ___ ___   a   b a g

boy at the grocery store. I 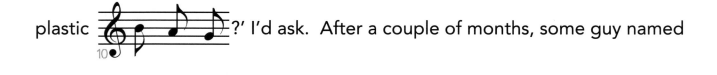 groceries late at night. 'Paper or

b a g g e d

plastic ?' I'd ask. After a couple of months, some guy named

___ ___ ___ ___

started working there, too, as 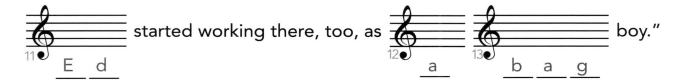 boy."

E d   a   b a g

[music notation 14] _ _ _ _ _ looked at [music notation 15] _ _. "Yes, that was me," said [music notation 16] .
E d

"We would always race to see who could [music notation 17] the fastest. Once, [music notation 18]
b a g   a

man came in the store and needed help. He saw the [music notation 19] on my
_ _ _ _ _

shirt. 'Can you help me, [music notation 20] ?' he asked. 'My wife [music notation 21] is
_ _ _   _ _ _ _

making dinner and needs [music notation 22] and [music notation 23]
c a b b a g e   b e e f

and an [music notation 24] for the cake. She [music notation 25] me to
e g g   _ _ _ _ _ _

come to the store, but I can't find anything!' I made a beeline for the

[music notation 26] , [music notation 27] went for the [music notation 28] ,
_ _ _ _ _ _   E d   b e e f

and we ran into each other by the [music notation 29] s." _ _ _ _ _ _ _ _
e g g

Goodbye

Bass Clef
Name the notes to spell missing words,
and spell underlined words by drawing notes on the staff.
Use eighth notes.   Remember the stem and flag rules.

"Uncle _____, it's been nice having you here," said _____. Her
1: E d   2: D e e D e e

mom and _____ agreed. "Can't you stay another day?" she
3: d a d

_____. "I'm sorry, _____, but I've got _____
4: _ _ _ _ _   5: _ _ _ _ _ _   6: _ _

wallet. _____ needs to go, too. It was great seeing you _____ to
7: A b e   8: f a c e

_____." _____ and her _____ loaded the
9: f a c e   10: _ _ _ _   11: _ _ _

_____ for _____ and _____ and
12: _ _ _ _ _ _   13: _ _ _   14: _ _ _

_____'s mom gave them _____ _____ of food. They
15: D e e D e e   16: a   17: b a g

watched as the car _____ into the distance.
18: _ _ _ _ _ _

Teacher or Parent Answer Guide

PAGE 8, Slick In Trouble

1. a   b a g   2. a   3. b e e   4. D a d   5. b e g g e d

6. b e g g e d   7. b e   8. G e e   9. D a d   10. f a c e

PAGE 9, Recipe No. 1—Cookies

1   2   3   4   5   6   7   8   9   10   11

PAGE 10, A Typical Day with Slick

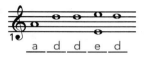

1. a d d e d   2. a   3. b e   4. f e d   5. f e d   6. f e d   7. a

8. a   9. b a g   10. b a g g a g e   11. a   12. b e a d   13. e d g e

14. b e g   15. b e   16. f e d   17. f a c e   18. b e d   19. a-sharp

PAGE 11, Recipe No. 2—Way Too Much Frosting

1. 6   2. 3   3. 12   4. 6   5. ½   6. 6   7. 2

PAGES 12 AND 13, Road Trip

1. E d   2. A b e   3. a   4. E d   5. a   6. D E   7. G A   8. D E   9. A b e

10. f e e d   11. f a c e   12. b e g g e d   13. E d   14. a   15. c a f e

16. a   17. d e a d   18. A d a   19. b e e f   20. e g g   21. b e e f   22. E d

23. a d d   24. a   25. e g g   26. A b e   27. b-flat   28. E d   29. d e a d

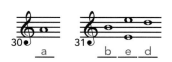

30. a   31. b e d

PAGE 14, Lightning Round No. 1

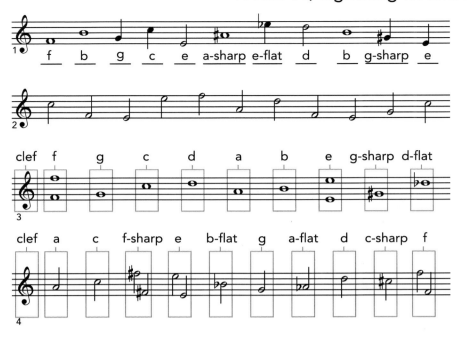

PAGE 15, Scavenger Hunt

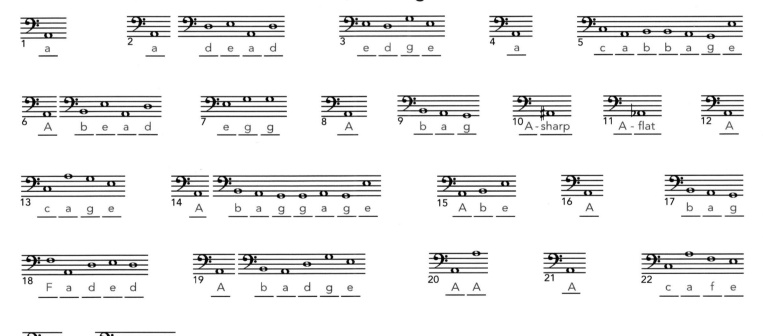

PAGE 16, The Visit

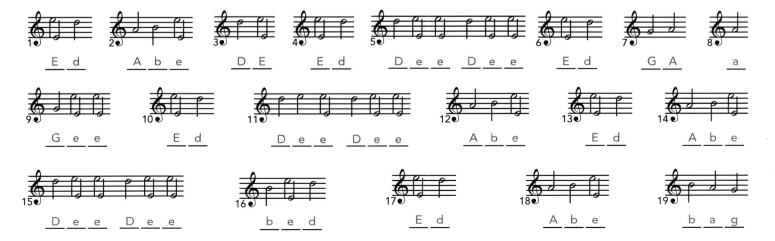

PAGE 17, The Card Game

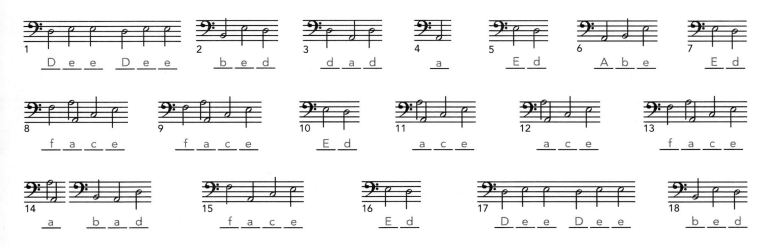

PAGE 18, Lightning Round #2

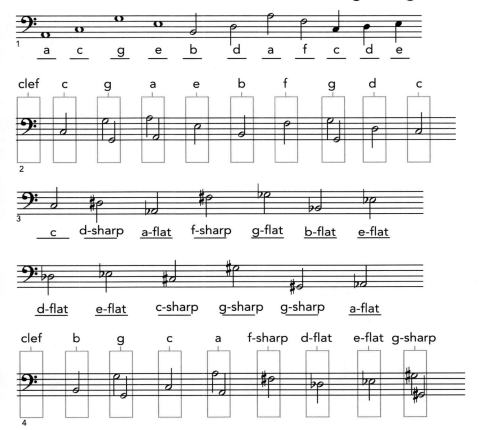

PAGE 19, The Zoo

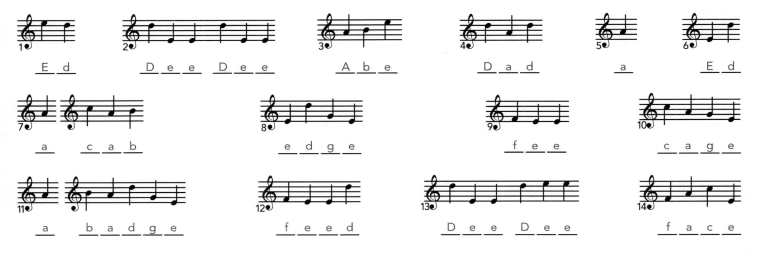

29

PAGE 20, A Good Deed

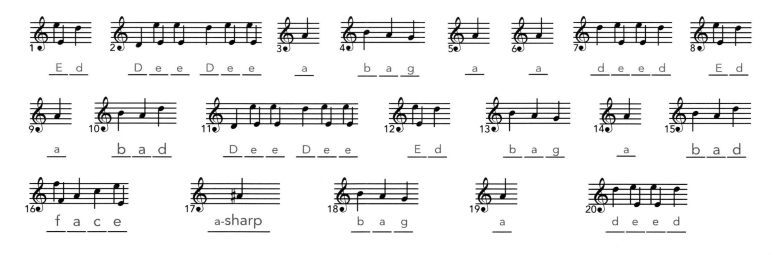

1	E d
2	D e e D e e
3	a
4	b a g
5	a
6	a
7	d e e d
8	E d
9	a
10	b a d
11	D e e D e e
12	E d
13	b a g
14	a
15	b a d
16	f a c e
17	a-sharp
18	b a g
19	a
20	d e e d

PAGE 21, The Post Office

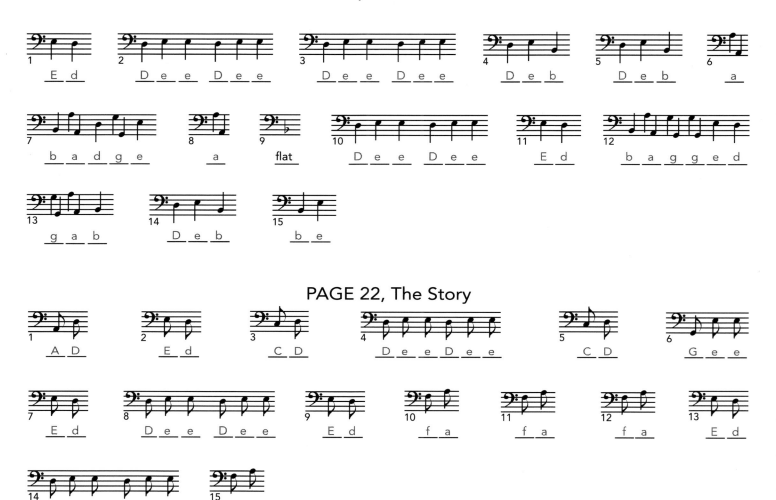

1	E d
2	D e e D e e
3	D e e D e e
4	D e b
5	D e b
6	a
7	b a d g e
8	a
9	flat
10	D e e D e e
11	E d
12	b a g g e d
13	g a b
14	D e b
15	b e

PAGE 22, The Story

1	A D
2	E d
3	C D
4	D e e D e e
5	C D
6	G e e
7	E d
8	D e e D e e
9	E d
10	f a
11	f a
12	f a
13	E d
14	D e e D e e
15	f a

PAGE 23, Lightning Round No. 3

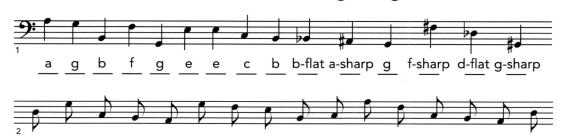

1. a g b f g e e c b b-flat a-sharp g f-sharp d-flat g-sharp

2. a

PAGE 23, Lightning Round No. 3, continued

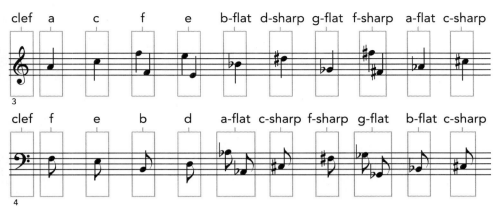

clef | a | c | f | e | b-flat | d-sharp | g-flat | f-sharp | a-flat | c-sharp

clef | f | e | b | d | a-flat | c-sharp | f-sharp | g-flat | b-flat | c-sharp

PAGE 24-25, The Bag Boy

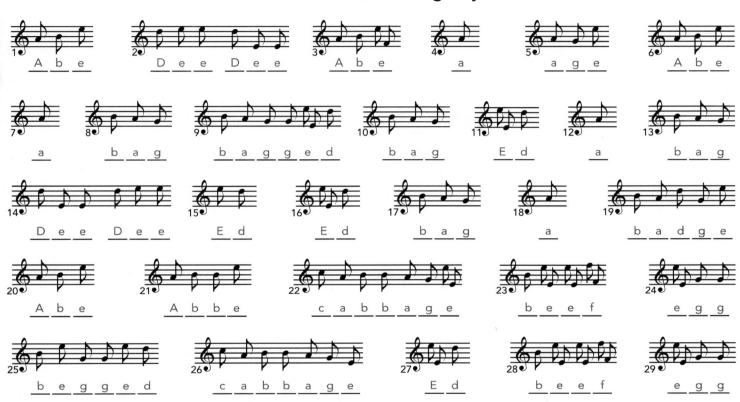

PAGE 26, Goodbye

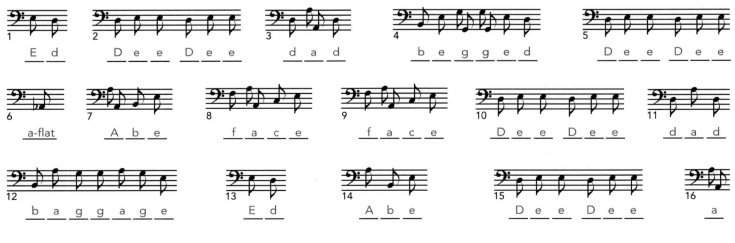